Hurricane Island

A True Story

Gloria Shaw Illustrated by Florence Miller

Key West, FL

This book is distributed to bookstores and libraries
through Ingram Book Company. www.ingrambook.com

Copyright © 2008
ISBN: 9780981812403
All rights reserved, etc.

VOLTAIRE BOOKS™
Key West, Florida
www.voltairebooks.com

Acknowledgements:

Thank you to Greg for providing the inspiration for this story.

I must thank and acknowledge Lois Kline for her patient help with the manuscript.

Gloria Shaw

This is a true story about a
Hurricane named Wilma and how
some folks in Key West made it
through, including
a lady named Gloria.

Key West is a very small island at the end of a 150-mile chain off the southern end of Florida.

Some people consider Key West paradise.

Gloria is one of those people.

Gloria lives in Old Town Key West in the back of a little church on a small hill called Solares Hill, the only hill in the Florida Keys.

Solares Hill is 19 feet above sea level, and most of Old Town is built there, proof that the early settlers were smart.

Every year, some hurricanes form over warm oceans, and people who live along coasts learn to watch for them in the summer—including Gloria.

One year, during the last warm days of October, a hurricane headed toward Key West.

It came from the central area of the Caribbean Sea and through the Gulf of Mexico pushing a *surge* of water ahead of it and flooding any land in its path.

Before a hurricane arrives, the weather experts (called meteorologists) give lots of information about the speed of the winds (categories) and the track (path) of the hurricane.

Hurricane Categories

1	**74-95 miles per hour (mph)** Damage to trees and mobile homes.
2	**96-110 mph** Roofs and windows damaged, some trees toppled.
3	**111-130 mph** Buildings and large trees blown down, flooding near shoreline, mobile homes destroyed.
4	**131-155 mph** Extensive damage to homes, doors, and windows, and damage to lower floors of houses near shoreline.
5	*(Gee Whiz!)* **More than 155 mph** Roofs and some buildings destroyed. Massive evacuations. All trees and signs blown down.

* Adapted from the National Weather Service: www.nws.noaa.gov

Meteorologists also provide a name for each hurricane. This one was called Wilma.

Wilma was a Category 3 hurricane.

The meteorologists issued a hurricane warning but not a mandatory evacuation.

Gloria had to think carefully about evacuating to the mainland or preparing for the storm at home.

Gloria decided she would stay on the island.

Her dogs stayed, too.

If a hurricane hits Key West, sometimes the electricity is turned off and sometimes the water, too.

People who stayed had to make sure they had:

- ❏ Bottled water
- ❏ Canned food
- ❏ Flashlights
- ❏ A battery-operated radio
- ❏ Extra batteries

Most houses in Key West have window shutters that people closed tight during the storm. The local stores put boards over their windows.

The day began sunny and breezy, and then the sky filled with dark clouds.

Then, WOW! Rain poured down and the wind roared and the trees were bent to the ground.

Gloria's dogs are scared of thunder. There was a lot of thunder and lightning during the hurricane, so the dogs hid under the bed.

Gloria thought she and the dogs were going to be fine, but she decided to move to a little room in the back of the church away from the windows just to be extra safe.

She put a bunch of pillows on the floor and placed the radio and flashlight next to her, and tried to sleep through the storm.

The dogs had no bed to climb under, so they snuggled close to Gloria to feel reassured.

Then the electricity shut off.

Gloria tuned the radio to the station that was still broadcasting information. Gloria grabbed the flashlight and began to inspect her house.

The wind was noisy and so strong that it beat the branches of a nearby tree against the roof. Water was leaking in around the doors and windows.

There was a loud THUMP! right above their heads, and the dogs began barking ferociously.

It was too dark to go outside, so Gloria told her dogs, "Hush! Let's try to get some sleep."

And eventually they did sleep.

In the morning, Gloria and her dogs went outside and looked around.

The big THUMP! had been a huge tree next door that had fallen on top of Gloria's roof—the *whole tree*.

"What a shame," Gloria said. The neighbors were sad, too, not just for the hole in the roof. The tree was a beautiful Royal Poinciana tree with lots of red blossoms.

The storm surge had flooded most of Key West, and as Gloria went around, she saw people dragging wet stuff out of their houses.

There was not a green leaf anywhere. The wind and rain had torn them all off.

Groups like FEMA (the Federal Emergency Management Agency) and the Red Cross came in with helicopters.

Soon, damaged roofs were covered with blue tarps to keep out the rain until they could be repaired.

Tree trimmers were all over town cutting fallen trees off of roofs and cleaning the streets.

It seemed that paradise would never be the same for Gloria.

But one year later, the island was beautiful again, trees had their leaves back, and the roofs around Old Town were all repaired.

That summer hurricane season came and went with NO hurricane.

And I came to Key West to visit my Grandma.

Grandma and I stood in Mallory Square—the best place to watch the sun set in Key West.

"What was it like during the hurricane?" I asked.

"First," Grandma said, "You must understand that this is paradise…"

Preparing for a Hurricane

- Monitor the weather and announcements related to the storm.

- Evacuate if told to do so.

- Make a family hurricane plan before you need to have one.

- Make sure your pets are part of your plan – they depend on you to keep them safe as well.

- Create a hurricane supply kit.

For more information about hurricane safety, visit www.nhc.noaa.gov

Sample Family Hurricane Plan

- Discuss the types of hazards that could affect your family.

- Know your home's vulnerability to storm surge, flooding and wind.

- Locate a safe room or the safest areas in your home for each hurricane hazard. In certain circumstances, the safest areas may not be your home but within your community.

- Determine escape routes from your home and places to meet.

- Have an out-of-state friend as a family contact, so all your family members have a single point-of-contact.

- Make a plan now for what to do with your pets if you need to evacuate.

- Post emergency telephone numbers by your phones and make sure your children know how and when to call 911.

- Check your insurance coverage - flood damage is not usually covered by homeowners insurance.

- Stock non-perishable emergency supplies and a hurricane supply kit.

- Use a NOAA weather radio. Remember to replace its battery every 6 months, as you do with your smoke detectors.

- Take first aid, CPR, and disaster preparedness classes.

Sample Hurricane Supply Kit

- **Water** - at least 1 gallon daily per person for 3 to 7 days

- **Food** - at least enough for 3 to 7 days

— non-perishable packaged or canned food / juices
— foods for infants or the elderly
— snack foods
— non-electric can opener
— cooking tools / fuel
— paper plates and plastic utensils
— pet food

- **Blankets / Pillows, etc.**

- **Clothing** - seasonal / rain gear / sturdy shoes

- **First Aid kit / Medicines / Prescription drugs**

- **Special Items** - for babies and the elderly

- **Toiletries / Hygiene items / Moisture wipes**

- **Flashlight / Batteries**

- **Radio** - Battery operated and NOAA weather radio

- **Telephones** - Fully-charged cell phone with extra battery and a traditional (not cordless) telephone set

- **Cash** (with some small bills) and **Credit cards** - Banks and ATMs may not be available for extended periods

- **Extra keys**

- **Toys/ Books / Games**

- **Important documents -** in a waterproof container or watertight re-sealable plastic bag
  — insurance, medical records, bank account numbers, Social Security card, Passport, etc.

- **Tools -** keep a set with you during the storm

- **Vehicle with fuel tanks filled**

Keep Your Pets Safe During a Hurricane

- A 3-day supply of food and drinking water, as well as bowls.

- Cats also need cat litter and a container to be used as a litter box.

- Current photos and descriptions of pets.

- Up-to-date identification, including an additional tag with the phone number of someone out of the area in the event the pet becomes lost.

- Medications, medical records and a First Aid Kit stored in a waterproof container.

- Sturdy leashes, harnesses, and carriers to transport pets safely as well as blankets or towels for bedding and warmth. Carriers should be large enough to comfortably house your pet for several hours or even days.

For more information about pets and hurricanes, visit www.hsus.org/disaster

Notes

Printed in the United States
120285LV00001B